T0348793

THE
ZERO
PRINCIPLE

Changing Lives,
One Mind at a Time

Richmond Brock, Jr.

ALSO, BY RICHMOND BROCK JR

WW3- The Reset

Fighting Back Against Big Business

The Brain Dormitory

Dedicated with every iota of my being,

resonating through the very fabric of time and space.

To my Father & Friend

Richmond Milton Brock Sr.

TABLE OF CONTENTS

INTRODUCTION

As you turn these pages, prepare to transcend beyond the ordinary. Be ready to challenge the boundaries of your thoughts, opening doors to uncharted territories of opportunity — both in the intimate corners of your personal life and the expansive arenas of your professional journey.

In the vast expanse of human existence, amidst the clamor of everyday life, lies an often unexplored realm of understanding and enlightenment. This isn't merely a book; it's a transformative expedition designed to recalibrate your life's compass.

Let go of preconceived notions. Embrace the enlightenment. Revel in newfound joys and clarity. You're not just reading a book; you're embarking on a voyage to unearth the profound truths of your very being.

Begin this journey and discover why you're truly here. Your odyssey to a transformed mindset, radiant with joy and purpose, starts now. Welcome to "The Zero Principle." Dive deep, for the treasures within!

CHAPTER ONE:
THE BALANCING ACT

The Zero Principle

Lead in your own direction instead of following others;
there are countless paths to success.

The universe has guaranteed all of us one thing in its entirety: a beginning with an end and an end with a guaranteed beginning. No matter how good or bad a situation may seem now, I remember that outcomes may change. I stopped worrying and comparing myself to others' achievements because I have personal winnings. I developed a polarity of conscious awareness and encourage others to do the same.

In my life, I had many people that I admired but never let their milestones become an unreachable ambition. I was determined to turn my dreams into reality. I had a realization that all humans are connected to the same source, and with this, I became empowered to create my destiny.

Growing up, things were different. Most of the kids in my neighborhood didn't seem to like me. There were times I felt low. I felt out of place, especially when my friends seemed smarter or better at sports. But then I noticed that usually, they were just better at one thing. That's when I realized that everyone has something they're good at. I decided to focus on what I could do best, and over time, I found my own place to shine.

The Zero Principle:

Every day is a brand-new life, just like that.

The Zero Principle helps me find peace in all situations, maintaining stability and balance. It is not about what I have or don't have; it's the understanding that this is just life in its entirety. The universe resets any situation, whether we see it as good or bad, because we're all part of the same existence. I've observed how nature resets itself continuously, like a seed from soil to a beautiful flower, then withers away, returns to soil, and rises like a Goddess. Every new sunrise is a brand-new life. I am granted a clean slate to choose whether to harbor yesterday's misfortunes or to move forward. I know that I have all the time in the world, depending on perspectives but I also must remind myself, the clock is ticking...

The Zero Principle:

Life continually resets itself, whether in social gatherings or personal experiences. Embrace these resets as opportunities for growth and understanding and let go of judgment.

Example:

1. For instance, you've been employed at your job for several years, and suddenly you get a promotion with new responsibilities, and now you're struggling with your job duties. This is a form of a 'reset' that life must continue to

"push" for you to grow. Then right when your job might become too complicated, life will give you a moment of clarity, and then suddenly, your job becomes "easy" again. I strayed away from what I thought was a positive or negative situation and started realizing this was just life.

2. You arrive at a house party or get-together around 6:30 pm, and everything is going well. People are in the corner conversing and laughing, and new relationships are forming, but then, someone drops a glass or breaks something, and the entire party stops for a few seconds. Then, just like that, the party starts back up again. **I started noticing that whenever a gathering is going too well, a reset must happen.** I no longer look at these instances as good or bad; instead, I strive to understand and observe *the* (Zero Principle) *natural law*.

The Zero Principle:

Understand that you are not seeking balance;
you are a continuous act of balancing.

Imagine life as a graph with a vertical line that runs from -10 to +10, with 0 in the middle, representing a state of "balance." My aim is to hover between negative (-3) and positive (+3). This way, I'm open to life's varied experiences, understanding that highs come with lows. I'm convinced that no one can truly achieve a state of perfect balance. But what we can strive for is a rhythm that acknowledges and embraces life's inevitable fluctuations.

Many people turn to gurus, books, and meditation in hopes of finding this balance, dreaming of a day when nothing can shake their calm or stir their emotions. But if you're so centered that nothing moves you—neither joy nor sorrow—you're missing out on the essence of being human. Being human means undergoing experiences that tug at our emotions, swinging us between elation and despair.

There's talk about humanity moving into the 4th and 5th dimensions with some feeling they're already transitioning to these higher states. But it's essential to remember that to ascend to these elevated planes, one must first navigate the lows, learning to lift one's consciousness. Often, it's the most challenging situations that lead to the most significant growth. Think of that job you never wanted but gave you your biggest break.

At every moment, you are in a state of balancing. Recognize that this balancing act is not external; it's your intrinsic power. So, embrace your journey and remember you are perfect in your imperfections.

CHAPTER TWO:
THE COLLECTIVE

The Zero Principle:

Recognize that our collective experiences often serve as mutual resets,
shaping our individual journeys.

The zero principle governs circumstances that might initially seem negative but can evolve for the better, or they might mirror day-to-day occurrences in our lives.

Consider this scenario:

Throughout the week, you've been driving recklessly, speeding even with your mom in the car, fully aware of her past traumatic experience with a major accident. Moreover, you've been consistently waking up late, rushing to work each morning in dread of tardiness. Then, Friday comes, and you rear-end someone's vehicle, resulting in a significant accident.

This collision wasn't just a random event; it echoed the cosmic repercussions of your preceding actions. Your imprudent driving jeopardizes your record, and you heavily rely on your car. Beyond that, there's the potential harm to an innocent person. Furthermore, your reckless behavior rekindled traumatic memories for your mom, who has always been supportive. The universe orchestrated this incident, possibly as a lesson urging you to pause and reassess multiple aspects of your life.

Let's also consider the individual whose car you hit. While it's easy to see this event as a misfortune, it's essential to understand that things don't merely happen to us; they happen for us. For this person, it might signal the need for a fresh start in a new city. It could be an eye-opener, making them reflect on their past actions towards others. Alternatively, the accident might have inadvertently solved a dilemma for the unsuspecting victim—young college student who was pressured into purchasing a new car. With her financial constraints due to her studies, the ensuing car payment and insurance could jeopardize her educational aspirations. Sometimes, the universe acts in mysterious ways, guiding individuals towards a more significant destiny even if they remain unaware of it. Once again, the zero principle comes into play here.

When your life seems to be flowing smoothly, there will always be little ripples, or something perceived as misfortune. It's how our mathematical universe maintains its intrinsic balance, resetting and recalibrating diverse aspects of our existence.

The Zero Principle:

The zero principle continuously asserts itself to ensure balance in all perspectives on Earth.

No one person holds all knowledge. A master in one domain might be a novice in another. Every individual, regardless of age, has unique insights to bring to the table. In our rapidly changing world, we now see young adults shaping the tech industry, offering fresh perspectives instead of relying solely on "temporary truths." Imagine if everyone collaboratively engaged in understanding our planet. Some may not excel in traditional math, but they possess unique talents, such as decoding patterns or visualizing complex concepts intuitively.

I have engaged in deep conversations with professionals; engineers, astrophysicist, and other scholars in their fields. They often wonder how I match their intellectual depth without a formal background in certain disciplines. I believe that the essence of every influential figure in history lingers with us - energy does not vanish. There is an interconnected energy grid enveloping us, a nexus through which every thought travels which some call the quantum realm or "Zero Point." My diverse interactions and willingness to learn from everyone have cultivated a rich repository of knowledge, spanning the entirety of human history. Today's scientific community is finally recognizing the value of unconventional thinkers like me.

While at the park, some parents, intrigued by my perspectives, questioned if I might be on the autism spectrum. I often describe myself as "autistic without autism." On my journey, I've observed that many on the spectrum or those with unconventional thinking patterns often perceive concepts that others might dismiss as mere fantasies. I believe many with autism possess forward-thinking, evolved minds. Instead of seeing their cognitive differences as deficiencies due to our limited understanding, we should learn from them, fostering growth and innovation. As we encounter challenges in understanding, let it serve as a reminder of the impending enlightenment. Continually strive for greater understanding rather than narrowly focusing on setbacks.

The Zero Principle:

Understanding neutrality for the sake of clarity and rebirth.

Returning to a neutral or "zero point" is not just a theoretical concept but a vital component of our human existence. At a quantum level, our bodies thrive and resonate within the zero-point quantum field. This state can be likened to the tranquility that follows a storm, the stillness succeeding chaos, or the silence after an uproar. Within this 'zero' state, there's a unique serenity that provides us with lucidity, unburdened by past regrets or anxieties about future undertakings. This pause, however fleeting, allows us to detach from emotions, biases, or preconceptions and perceive things in their true form. When immersed in this zero-consciousness state, the peaceful sensation accelerates the already charged protons, rejuvenating, and cleansing our energy field at light speed.

The elegance of the zero principle emerges from its sheer simplicity. By recognizing that we perpetually possess the chance to circle back to this foundational balance, we can tackle life's hurdles with enhanced poise and fortitude. This principle is like erasing a board, allowing us to release the past and welcome the potential of the future. In these instances of recentering, we discover opportunities for renewal and transformation.

Furthermore, this principle teaches us the value of humility. In a world that often pushes us to extremes, the zero principle serves as a reminder that in the vast expanse of the universe, we are but a fleeting moment. And yet, within that moment lies infinite potential. By embracing the 'zero,' we accept the impermanence of life and the ever-changing nature of existence, finding peace in the knowledge that, regardless of where we stand today, tomorrow offers a new beginning.

CHAPTER THREE:
"ZERO POINT"

The Zero Principle:

Refrain from passing judgment on individuals,
as there may come a day when you rely on their support.

Consider the sister who often swears or indulges in too much alcohol. She might be the very same person who steps up to shelter a wayward niece or nephew, setting them on a path to stability-helping them enroll in school and securing them a job. Sometimes, what we see as a person's flaws can turn out to be their strengths in specific contexts.

Take my maternal family as an example. My relatives hail from England, well-educated and sharp-minded. My grandmother, a nurse, moved to Cupertino, California in the 1980s an upscale region even today, nestled close to posh Palo Alto. Yet, amidst this affluence, my youngest aunt, at the age of twenty, was introduced to the world of cocaine at a high-end party. This was an era when the less fortunate were becoming entangled with a much cheaper and a lot more dangerous version of cocaine (crack cocaine), while the affluent indulged in its costly counterpart. Surrounded by affluence, my aunt felt at ease and said, "Sure, why not." This decision set her on a path from cocaine to crystal methamphetamine over a twenty year time span. Receiving constant ridicule from her siblings, she eventually fled the region, moving to a different city and leaving her past behind.

Here's where the zero principle comes into play:

Fast forward to the early 2000's and my grandmother's final days, battling ovarian cancer. While her children made fleeting visits, citing work or other commitments, she was prepared to stay indefinitely. Yet, it was the same "addicted" aunt who insisted that everyone else could leave and she would remain with "Mummy." Shockingly, most didn't take time off work, some even holding underlying relief about her impending departure. However, this aunt, whom many had written off, stayed sober, displaying profound love, dedication respect and patience, right up until my grandmother's last moment.

The very person many labeled a thief, and a liar was the only one present in our family's hour of need. And, that person that you once dismissed and marginalized ends up embodying a person of deep character and resilience. This story serves as a poignant reminder: when we judge others, we might eventually find ourselves in the same shoes we once criticized.

The Zero Principle:

Avoid matching a person's frequency, as it can ensnare you in their realm. Let them expend their energy while your current remains as strong as when the interaction began.

Along my journey, I learned to accept things as they are and just be. If a person is acting in a certain way, I accept it. Their energy is no more powerful than mine so I will let it run its temporary course. Although it might seem as if I'm not in control, the real power lies in allowing them to think they have control by letting them exert all their energy first as I retune my frequency. Now I have positioned myself in a state of awareness instead of compulsiveness, which is a form of non-control.

It's wise to always maintain your frequency instead of lowering it to meet someone where they're operating. By lowering your frequency of engaging in low vibrational acts such as anger, hate, frustration, fear, etc. you put yourself at risk of possibly dwelling in it longer than you would like. Instead, if you maintain your high vibration, you can influence and transmute their low vibrational frequency.

The Zero Principle:

Try new things that you didn't initially enjoy. By becoming proficient at them, you'll excel when you return to what you love.

I set my intentions on becoming the best at things I didn't enjoy. Becoming good at something that I didn't like allowed me to grow exponentially with the added benefit of combating the ego, which is driven only by my wants and desires. I threw out my beliefs that I had to love what I did to succeed. Often, pushing myself beyond my limits gave me a greater understanding of something new, that initially presented itself as a dislike. To achieve something, I had to try my hardest consistently. I didn't worry about the results or whether my wants or desires were fulfilled, because regardless, it always ended in a win-win situation. All my efforts spawned a new level of understanding, diligence, perseverance, and resilience that I might have never had if I didn't try and fail.

On the contrary, when I didn't try, a non-trying attitude developed, and I realized how much I didn't like the person I was becoming. As a result, my brain's survival mode activated in attempts to figure out how to maneuver out of the mindset. Fortunately, something is always gained—whether it's the wisdom about how I love myself or how much I don't love myself. I had to bring myself into awareness and get out of thinking that I already knew everything in my profession or daily life. I knew that if I did not shift my mindstate, it would have stunted my learning growth, leading to stagnation and complacency. *We must remember that we are students of the universe, there is always something we can explore.*

CHAPTER FOUR:
NO-IMPOSSIBLE

The Zero Principle:

"You become what you believe."

Phrases like "Life's a grind, then it ends," "Just do it without overthinking," and "What's meant to be, will be," were commonly heard during my upbringing and remain popular today. While these statements often come from a place of self-motivation, they can also resonate as undeniable truths. But every truth, in my experience, has close relatives: belief, faith, and hope. In my forty-six years, the one constant I have found is faith.

Faith isn't something I can visually observe or stash in my wallet. It's trusting in HOPE without tangible evidence. Backed by deliberate actions, this trust deepened into FAITH. And even when my aspirations seemed unattainable, faith-fueled my persistence. As I've achieved my goals, my BELIEFS have solidified. It's important to clarify that I'm not referencing religious connotations, though the concept can be relevant in that context as well. Even though your beliefs might change you have another new understanding of the Impossible being possible. Always remember, stumbling blocks and setbacks are often just a step removed from success.

The Zero Principle:

What's destined to happen will undoubtedly occur.
Even if it's just once, don't abandon your hope.

Imagine you're the smallest kid on the football team. You might not be the strongest, but a family member always told you to hold onto the faith that you could achieve greatness. Your heart beats for football, and even though the odds seem stacked against you, you made the team because you were the fastest during tryouts. Every day since, you've pushed yourself, working twice as hard as anyone else, trying to make the most of your time on the field. Your family faithfully shows up to nearly every game, hoping to witness the moment their son shines.

That long-awaited moment arrives during the championship playoff game. With the star receiver sidelined due to injury, an unexpected door of opportunity swings open. You, who spent most of the season on the sidelines, are suddenly thrust into the limelight. The coach, in a pivotal decision, calls your name, recognizing that your speed might be the team's last shot at victory. The chosen play is the "Hail Mary," a desperate but hopeful strategy where the quarterback throws the ball as far as possible, relying on the fastest player on the field to make that crucial catch. It's an awe-inspiring turn of events as the one who had been overlooked all season becomes the secret weapon for the football team's victory. Always remember to persist and stay on the course. The universe will ensure that at least once, you'll have your moment to shine, matching or even surpassing the prowess of others in your unique way.

The Zero Principle:

Understand that there is no ceiling or "highest level." You can and will always surpass your limits if you simply keep moving forward.

A good friend of mine Tyree told me one day: *"Richmond, you know what going hard is. When you are going your hardest (gym, studies, etc.), you start going harder than that! Now, you're just starting to go hard."*

My personal analogy: Let us say I can only do a maximum amount (twenty) of push-ups, and at the seventeenth rep and eighteenth rep, I am digging into every bit of my life force within me to do the last two repetitions. At this moment, on my nineteenth rep, I want to tell myself, *"Richmond come on, you can do it; keep going,"* forcing myself to create the possible out of an impossible thought. Now on the twenty-second rep, I can feel the rocket fuel of strength and power. I have now created a stronger Richmond entirely; **the impossible is always possible.** If I surrender to my impossible thoughts and keep going, I will keep moving forward.

The Zero Principle

When you fail at something, reward yourself instead of ridicule, and you won't mind failing as a means of learning.
The ultimate truth is zero, undefined.

Life's meaning is in constant flux, and so is our perceptions. Success should be seen as fleeting victories, while failure should be recognized as valuable insights. When you stumble, instead of getting upset, reflect on the lessons. Every setback offers a chance to think differently and explore avenues you hadn't considered before. Avoiding failures can lead to a standstill, often creating an illusion of stability or safety. Be brave, keep moving, and free yourself from overthinking. While it's always good to plan, acting is key. Mere contemplation can be paralyzing, causing you to get trapped in a cycle of procrastination. Time will fly, and you might end up with a list of reasons for unmet goals. As you navigate through life's challenges, you become more resilient and understanding, making your time on Earth even more enriching.

LAWS OF THE ZERO PRINCIPLE:

The Zero Principle: *Lead in your own direction instead of following others; there are countless paths to success.*

The Zero Principle: *Every day is a brand-new life, just like that.*

The Zero Principle: *Life continually resets itself, whether in social gatherings or personal experiences. Embrace these resets as opportunities for growth and understanding letting go of judgment.*

The Zero Principle: *Understand that you are not seeking balance; you are a continuous, active balancing.*

The Zero Principle: *Recognize that our collective experiences often serve as mutual resets, shaping our individual journeys.*

The Zero Principle: *The zero principle continually asserts itself to ensure balance, in all perspectives on earth.*

The Zero Principle: *Understanding neutrality for the sake of clarity and rebirth.*

The Zero Principle: *Refrain from passing judgment on individuals, as there may come a day when you rely on their support.*

The Zero Principle: *Avoid matching a person's frequency, as it can trap you in their realm. Let them expend their energy while your own remains as strong as when the interaction began.*

The Zero Principle: *Try new things that you didn't initially enjoy. By becoming proficient at them, you'll excel when you return to what you love.*

The Zero Principle: *"You become what you believe."*

The Zero Principle: *What's destined to happen will undoubtedly occur. Even if it's just once, don't abandon your hope.*

The Zero Principle: *Understand that there is no ceiling or "highest level." You can and will continually surpass your limits if you keep moving forward.*

The Zero Principle: *When you fail at something, reward yourself instead of ridicule, and you won't mind failing as a means of learning. The ultimate truth is zero, undefined.*

Now that you've delved into the Zero Principle and explored its wisdom, take a moment to connect with your inner self. Which of these Zero Principles resonates most deeply with your heart and soul? Pause and reflect on the insights you've gained from this journey.

Time for change!

Pick one of Richmond Brock's Zero Principles that stood out to you the most. Now that you understand the Laws of the Zero Principle how might that situation be different? What can you do in the future to think differently when a situation like this arises? What did this Zero Law do to change the way you look at life, people, or situations?

* *

WORKBOOKS

"0 Point" Exercises

Exercise #1:

Instructions:

{Section A}

Step 1:

1. Locate a quiet and cozy spot. Ready a blank sheet or utilize the provided note pages.

2. At the top, jot down one trait or characteristic about yourself that you have viewed negatively at times.

Step 2:

1. After noting it down, take a brief pause, and shut your eyes.

2. Breathing only through your mouth, take a full breath in and a full breath out, counting down from twenty. During this time, focus your thoughts on the aspect you've written down.

Step 3:

1. Consider the two sides of this trait. Ask your inner self or the deeper consciousness: How has this trait been helpful or beneficial in different moments of your life?

2. Reflection is vital. Dive into your memories, rewinding through life's scenes, and remember occasions when this trait positively influenced you.

_____

_____

_____

_____

_____

_____

_____

_____

_____

_____

_____

_____

_____

_____

_____

_____

_____

_____

_____

_____

{PART B}

Step 1:

1. Reflect on two more traits or characteristics of yourself. If you'd like a deeper exploration of reshaping your self-view, think about doing this exercise for up to six traits, or however many you're at ease with.

2. Allow yourself ample time during this introspection; think of this as your "0 point."

Explanation:

This exercise is designed to boost the frontal cortex of your brain. It guides your mind in discerning which version of "you" fits best in various situations, and how to adjust when it might not be ideal. These practices will offer you clearer insights into your choices, boundaries, and adaptabilities in diverse situations and/or circumstances.

If we simply label things as "good" or "bad," our eyes will see them that way. But when you present your mind with nuanced insights about how you'd like it to act, it can work at its best to match your goals in different situations.

Engaging in self-reflection gives your brain richer information to process. The primary goal here is to set the "0 point," meaning you don't let your brain favor one side of you more than another. Some might see this as cultivating equilibrium.

Always remember: A trait you value highly in one setting might be less favorable in another. Conversely, what you view as a challenge or weakness might shine as a strength under different lights.

Examples:

Negative: Feeling inadequate

Positive: Pushed me to work harder, read more, and acquire knowledge, leading to empowerment.

Negative: Stubbornness or wanting things my way

Positive: Allows me to think outside the box, free from others' constraints. Recognizing there's no single "smartest" approach.

Negative: Feeling not smart enough

Positive: Instilled a proactive "just do it" attitude instead of complacency.

Negative: Experiencing bad luck

Positive: Believing that good luck is on the horizon.

Negative: Constantly restarting or beginning anew

Positive: Treating every day as a new opportunity and never surrendering hope.

Negative: Anger issues

Positive: Being assertive and standing up for yourself.

Negative: Being labeled as picky or too detailed

Positive: Knowing exactly what I want and refusing to compromise my standards.

Negative: Feeling like things never go my way

Positive: Trusting that my moment will arrive, so I need to be prepared.

Negative: OCD tendencies

Positive: Applying consistent care and attention to all areas of life, be it work, home, or finances.

Negative: Seen by others as conceited

Positive: Recognizing and valuing my self-worth and wanting the best for myself.

Negative: Perceived as overly serious

Positive: Taking opportunities with gravity to evaluate all possibilities.

Exercise #2:

Transforming Relationships

Step 1:

Think of a person in your life for whatever reason you feel treated you poorly and/or has done things to you that have hurt your feelings.

Step 2:

Vertically fold a piece of paper into two columns. On one column, jot down six or seven instances where this person directly or indirectly impacted you negatively.

Examples:

(Challenges)

1. They were extremely frugal, always prioritizing budget over enjoyment.

2. My mom's overprotectiveness limited my freedom during my younger years.

3. My dad, a preacher, sometimes spoke negatively about people, contradicting his spiritual role.

4. She constantly nagged me about life.

Remember, when people criticize you, they often reveal their own insecurities and self-perceived shortcomings. The next time someone attempts to confront you in a hostile manner, simply nod and smile, knowing that their words reflect more about them than they do about you.

Step 3:

On the other column, reflect on how these experiences, though challenging, have contributed to your personal growth.

(Contrast):

1. Such challenges echoed the belief, "better days ahead," guiding me to manage daily responsibilities while cherishing life's moments.

2. Promoted introspection and self-awareness, helping me to fortify my essence, undistracted by the external world's noise.

3. Instilled the value of not being judgmental. Accepting that no day is perfect.

4. They taught me to absorb lessons from others, filing them away in my mind for future reference.

(Growth Opportunities)

Scenario 1:

Now, fast forward three years, and you're purchasing your first condo or achieving something significant. Surprisingly, you realize that this person inadvertently taught you valuable financial lessons, even if their approach seemed overly stringent. You've learned to handle money wisely and explore investment opportunities.

Scenario 2:

Through their critical nature, this person indirectly instilled in you the importance of paying attention to minor details, which, left unattended, can escalate into significant issues. You've developed the skill of examining the micro aspects of situations, not just the macro details.

Scenario 3:

Reflecting on your sheltered upbringing, you acknowledge that it might have played a crucial role in your current achievements, such as nearing college graduation or establishing a strong sense of self that doesn't rely on external validation.

Scenario 4:

Your father's imperfections taught you the universal truth that nobody is flawless, whether they are a spiritual leader or an ordinary person. This experience reinforced the importance of faith and staying committed to what is morally right, even in the face of occasional missteps.

Exercise #3:
Lessons from Relationships

Objective: Harness your heightened self-awareness to derive insights from interactions with others.

Instructions:

1. **Selection of the Individual:** Begin by thinking about someone significant in your life, past or present. This could be a friend, family member, colleague, or even someone you met briefly but left a lasting impression.

2. **Reflection:** Sit comfortably, take a few deep breaths, and reflect on your relationship with this person. Delve into the interactions, conversations, and moments you've shared.

3. **Identify the Lesson:** Write down one valuable lesson that this individual has taught you. It doesn't need to be something they explicitly told you; it could be a lesson derived from their actions, habits, worldview, or simply their presence in your life.

4. **Detail the Influence:** Expand on how this lesson has influenced or changed you. How have you integrated this lesson into your life? How has it benefited you or those around you?

5. **Appreciation:** End the exercise with a moment of gratitude. Regardless of the nature of your relationship with this person, acknowledge the positive influence they've had on your personal growth journey.

Note: Remember, every individual we cross paths with can offer us a lesson. Sometimes, the most profound insights come from the most unexpected sources. Embrace each relationship as an opportunity for growth and self-discovery.

More Examples:

1. While you may have wished for a closer relationship with your mother, your time spent with your significant other taught you the true meaning of family. Observing their family gatherings makes you realize that every family faces its share of drama, ups, and downs, but they can agree to disagree. The most profound lesson was witnessing their unwavering commitment to each other, providing love and support, regardless of the day's conflicts.

2. The person introduced you to the world of entrepreneurship and successful business management, expanding your horizons.

3. Despite multiple failures, you gained the resilience to never stop trying, inspired by their determination.

4. This individual taught you the importance of setting boundaries and recognizing the distinctions between co-workers, acquaintances, and true friends.

5. They showed you the value of prioritizing self-care even when dealing with someone else's selfish behavior.

6. Their guidance made you a better parent, sibling, aunty or uncle.

7. They connected you with valuable resources and introduced you to important people in your life.

8. If you consider yourself an introvert, this person encourages you to step out of your comfort zone.

9. During a dark and hopeless period in your life, this person may not have been what you expected, but their daily laughter and support carried you through the toughest times.

What's important to understand is that, upon reflection, each of these relationships brought at least one valuable lesson for your future. Regardless of how challenging or negative the overall experience might have been, there's always at least one positive lesson that weighed as heavily or even more heavily than all the difficult times with that person. This lesson aligns with the Zero Principle, emphasizing that even in seemingly negative experiences, there is something to gain that contributes to your growth and development.

Blank Pages for Exercises

Please, consider sharing this book with someone who needs immediate life transformation. "The Zero Principle" is a valuable resource for the young or older person, who needs a reminder that every sunrise brings a fresh start. Yesterday may be in the past, but it serves as a steppingstone for a brighter future!

Your act of passing on "The Zero Principle" is a powerful contribution to the healing journey of all living beings on Earth. You are joining the mission initiated by a select few to elevate consciousness and wisdom across our planet.

Volume One
The Laws of the Zero Principle
This is only the beginning of your journey
into the Laws of the Zero.
And don't forget to do your exercises!

Thank you once again,
and please know that my love for you extends eternally.
Love and Light,
Richmond Brock